The Ultimate Film Quiz Book

By Steve & Kate Haywood

Copyright © 2021 Kate & Steve Haywood

All rights reserved.

Contents

Contents 3

Introduction 7

Film Quotes 9

Holidays & Events 11

Find the Links! 13

Fill in the Blanks 15

2010s Films 17

James Bond Films 19

Kate Winslet 21

US Film States 23

Disney Films 25

Sci-fi Films 27

2000s Films 29

Cities on Film 31

Children's Films 33

1990s films 35

Film Star Clues 37

Superheroes 39

Animals on Film 41

Harrison Ford Films	43
Film descriptions	45
1980s Films	47
Film Anagrams	49
Guess the Film	51
Romantic Comedies	53
1970s Films	55
Colours	57
Number Films	59
Real Star Names	61
Three English Dames	63
1960s Films	65
Missing Vowels	67
Harry Potter	69
More Anagrams	71
A Bit of a Mix	73
More Film Descriptions	75
1950s Films	77
Morgan Freeman	79
Marvel Actors	81
Gone Too Soon	83

More of a Mix 85

Real or Fake 87

A Trio of Characters 89

1930s & 1940s Films 91

More Film Star Clues 93

Tagines 95

Title Translations 97

Chicken or Egg 99

Famous Last Lines 101

Find the Links Again 103

Introduction

Welcome to The Ultimate Film Quiz Book with hundreds of different questions to enjoy as you spin through the films of past and present. There are questions of various types and styles, set to test your film knowledge to the limits. Perfect for any film buff and still great fun for those who don't pre-book their tickets for the big new releases the second they come out. So, sit back, relax and enjoy putting your film knowledge to the test. We hope you enjoy this book, do check out our other titles for more quizzing fun.

Also, if you like the books, do look at the other books we've got available. Visit our website at quiziclebooks.com for more details and to sign up for our newsletter – plus we're offering a **completely FREE subscriber only quiz book** when you sign up. There's also our Facebook page which is a great place to keep up with what we've got going on – just head on over to facebook.com/quiziclebooks.

Happy Quizzing!

Kate & Steve

Film Quotes

Everyone loves a film quote. Can you identify the films that these quotes are from?

1. A census taker once tried to test me. I ate his liver with some fava beans and a nice Chianti (1991)
2. I'll have what she's having (1989)
3. Love means never having to say you're sorry (1970)
4. I'll get you, my pretty, and your little dog, too! (1939)
5. We'll always have Paris (1942)
6. I love the smell of napalm in the morning. (1979)
7. I am big! It's the pictures that got small. (1950)
8. I'm also just a girl, standing in front of a boy, asking him to love her. (1999)
9. I'm just one stomach flu away from my goal weight. (2006)
10. If you let my daughter go now, that'll be the end of it. I will not look for you, I will not pursue you. But if you don't, I will look for you, I will find you, and I will kill you. (2008)
11. Badges? We ain't got no badges! We don't need no badges! I don't have to show you any stinking badges! (1948)
12. You had me at hello (1996)

Answers – Film Quotes

1. *The Silence of the Lambs*
2. *When Harry Met Sally*
3. *Love Story*
4. *The Wizard of Oz*
5. *Casablanca*
6. *Apocalypse Now*
7. *Sunset Boulevard*
8. *Notting Hill*
9. *The Devil Wears Prada*
10. *Taken*
11. *The Treasure of the Sierra Madre*
12. *Jerry Maguire*

Holidays & Events

Test your knowledge of film holidays and events

1. *Easter Parade* starred Judy Garland and Fred Astaire but who created the music?
2. In *Stakeout*, Maria McGuire's birthday is on the Day of the Dead. Who plays her?
3. Film *The Holiday* is about which holiday?
4. How many couples get married during *Four Weddings and a Funeral* (not the end credits!)?
5. The 2010 film *Valentine's Day* featured Julia Roberts and was released in the US on what date, 12th February, 13th February or 14th February?
6. Who is the *Father of the Bride* in the 1991 film?
7. What is the name of the actress who plays the birthday girl in the 1984 film *Sixteen Candles*?
8. In the *Twilight* Saga, who is Bella's husband?
9. *Trading Places* features Eddie Murphy as Billy Ray Valentine, but culminates during which other annual event?
10. Which 'holiday' film is a biopic about Ron Kovic who becomes anti-war and a pro-human rights activist after being paralysed in the Vietnam War?
11. In the 1975 Australian mystery *Picnic at Hanging Rock*, several girls and their teacher do what on Valentine's Day?
12. *It's a Wonderful Life* is a Christmas themed story from which decade?

Answers – Holidays & Events

1. Irving Berlin
2. Madeleine Stowe
3. Christmas
4. Three
5. 12th February, a Friday. All US movie theatre releases are on a Friday
6. Steve Martin
7. Molly Ringwald
8. Edward Cullen
9. New Year's Eve
10. *Born on the Fourth of July*
11. Disappear
12. 1940's

Find the Links!

Can you find what links these films? They could be a director, actor/actress, or not even a person at all!

1. *The Best Exotic Marigold Hotel, Love Actually, Arthur Christmas, and Pirates of the Caribbean: At World's End*
2. *The King's Speech, Charlie and the Chocolate Factory & Harry Potter and the Order of the Phoenix*
3. *From Here to Eternity, The Island of Dr. Moreau, Gunfight at the O.K. Corral & The Unforgiven*
4. *Natural Born Killers, Johnny Be Good, U.S. Marshalls, Avengers Assemble*
5. *Boogie Nights, The Graduate, Milk, Vertigo*
6. *The Evil Dead, The Gift, The Quick and the Dead, Spider-Man*
7. *Gladiator, The Golden Compass, The History of Love, Endgame*
8. *No Country for Old Men, Nanny McPhee, Gosford Park & Finding Neverland*
9. *Eat Pray Love, Midnight Express, Catch Me If You Can, Erin Brockovich*
10. *Enemy of the State, Ali, Bad Boys, Independence Day*

Answers – Find the Links!

1. Bill Nighy
2. Helena Bonham Carter
3. Burt Lancaster
4. Robert Downey Jr.
5. They all set in California
6. Sam Raimi, director
7. Derek Jacobi
8. Kelly Macdonald
9. They are all based on a true story
10. Will Smith

Fill in the Blanks

We've taken some words out of these movie titles. Can you fill in the blanks to reveal the answer? We've included the year of the film to give you a helping hand.

1. The _____, The _____ and The _____ (1966)
2. The ____ Hill _____ (1951)
3. ____ _____ One Night (1934)
4. The ____ Red ____ (1998)
5. He's Just ____ That ____ ____ (2009)
6. ____ ____ Lose ____ ____ ____ 10 ____ (2003)
7. The ___ ____ Rises (1957)
8. ____ Long ____ Goodnight (1996)
9. The ____ of Drunken _____ (1994)
10. Six ____ Seven ____ (1998)
11. Don't ____ _____ the _____ Dead (1991)
12. Night ____ _____ ____ Dead (1968)

Answers - Fill in the Blanks

1. *The Good, The Bad and The Ugly*
2. *The Lavender Hill Mob*
3. *It Happened One Night*
4. *The Thin Red Line*
5. *He's Just Not That into You*
6. *How To Lose a Guy in 10 Days*
7. *The Sun Also Rises*
8. *The Long Kiss Goodnight*
9. *The Legend of Drunken Master* (it's a Jackie Chan movie in case you were wondering)
10. *Six Days Seven Nights*
11. *Don't Tell Mum the Babysitter's Dead*
12. *Night of the Living Dead*

2010s Films

Can you answer these questions on films 2010-2019?

1. Films about Mars are typically flops, but which 2015 film about Mars was a big hit?
2. What is the sequel to 2018 film *Venom* starring Tom Hardy called?
3. The Social Network featured Jesse Eisenberg as which high profile public figure?
4. Which cast member of *Dunkirk* is better known as a famous singer?
5. Which actor who voiced Maui in *Moana*, believes voice acting is challenging and gets annoyed when celebrities are cast in voice films and do it badly?
6. *The Imitation Game* is based on the real code breakers of Bletchley Park during World War II and depicts which brilliant Mathematician?
7. In *12 Years a Slave*, Solomon Northup plays which instrument professionally before being kidnapped?
8. 2018 film *Bohemian Rhapsody* was first announced in 2010, who was originally cast as Freddie Mercury?
9. Name the 2013 film directed by Baz Luhrmann with Carey Mulligan as Daisy?
10. Which 2018 film, nominated for 5 Academy Awards was written and directed by Greta Gerwig?

Answers - 2010s Films

1. *The Martian*
2. *Venom: Let There Be Carnage*
3. Mark Zuckerberg
4. Harry Styles from One Direction
5. Dwayne Johnson (The Rock)
6. Alan Turing
7. Violin
8. Sacha Baron Cohen
9. *The Great Gatsby*
10. *Lady Bird*

James Bond Films

A huge set of films spanning 60 years, James Bond is a favourite character among the old and young alike. Let these films test your knowledge of 007.

1. Shirley Bassey sung the theme song to *Goldfinger*, *Diamonds are Forever* and which other Bond film?
2. As of 2017, which two actors have played James Bond on seven occasions?
3. What is Bond's favourite drink, and how does he like it?
4. Who was the villain in *Diamonds are Forever*?
5. In what year was the first Bond film, *Dr No*, released?
6. What was the first film to show James Bond driving his famous Aston Martin?
7. Two Bond films were released in 1983. What were they?
8. What was George Lazenby's only outing as James Bond?
9. What iconic character did Richard Kiel play in two James Bond films?
10. Who is the creator of James Bond, and author of the books on which most Bond films are based?
11. Who played Q in 17 Bond films?
12. Who sang the theme tune for 2021 film *No Time to Die*?

Answers - James Bond Films

1. *Moonraker*
2. Roger Moore and Sean Connery (although one wasn't considered an official Bond film)
3. Martini – shaken, not stirred
4. Blofeld
5. 1962
6. *Goldfinger*
7. *Octopussy* and *Never Say Never Again*. The latter was a remake of *Thunderball*. It starred Sean Connery, but was not considered an official James Bond film (it was made by a different company).
8. *On Her Majesty's Secret Service*
9. Jaws – he played the role in *The Spy Who Loved Me* and *Moonraker*
10. Ian Fleming
11. Desmond Llewelyn. He has appeared in more Bond films than any other actor. Factoid: Q stands for Quartermaster, Q's role in the films.
12. Billie Eilish

Kate Winslet

How well do you know Kate's films?

1. Kate Winslet played Marianne Dashwood in which 1995 adaptation of a Jane Austen novel?
2. In which 2002 fantasy blockbuster was she offered a part in but turned it down, the role being later given to Miranda Otto?
3. Winslet played Joanna Hoffman, the right-hand woman of the title character in which 2015 biopic?
4. What was the name of her character in the 1997 blockbuster *Titanic*?
5. What year was she born – 1970, 1975 or 1980?
6. Winslet's first acting job was dancing with the cookie monster in a TV advert for what cereal?
7. In what 1994 film did Kate Winslet make her big screen debut?
8. What character did she play in the 1994 film adaptation of *Hamlet*?
9. What film, based on a Richard Yates novel, did she play the character of April Wheeler?
10. For what 2008 film did she win a best actress Oscar?
11. In what 2003 film did she star alongside Kevin Spacey and Laura Linney?
12. In whose court did she play Princess Sarah in the 1995 comedy adventure?

Answers – Kate Winslet

1. *Sense and Sensibility*
2. *Lord of the Rings: The Two Towers*
3. *Steve Jobs*
4. *Rose*
5. *1975*
6. *Sugar Puffs*
7. *Heavenly Creatures*
8. *Ophelia*
9. *Revolutionary Road*
10. *The Reader*
11. *The Life of David Gale*
12. *(A Kid in) King Arthur's Court*

US Film States

These are all iconic films that in some way or other show off a particular US state. Some of the films may be set in more than one state, but we've picked the ones they are best known for.

1. *To Kill a Mockingbird*
2. *Gone with the Wind*
3. *The Wizard of Oz*
4. *A River Runs Through It*
5. *Chinatown*
6. *Ferris Bueller's Day Off*
7. *High Noon*
8. *Rocky*
9. *The Shining*
10. *Donnie Darko*
11. *Brokeback Mountain*
12. *The Stepford Wives*
13. *Pearl Harbour*
14. *The Notebook*
15. *Cape Fear*

Answers - US Film States

1. *To Kill a Mockingbird* – Alabama
2. *Gone with the Wind* – Georgia
3. *The Wizard of Oz* – Kansas
4. *A River Runs Through It* - Montana
5. *Chinatown* – California
6. *Ferris Bueller's Day Off* - Illinois
7. *High Noon* – New Mexico
8. *Rocky* –Pennsylvania
9. *The Shining* – Colorado
10. *Donnie Darko* – Virginia
11. *Brokeback Mountain* – Wyoming
12. *The Stepford Wives* – Connecticut
13. *Pearl Harbour* – Hawaii
14. *The Notebook* – South Carolina
15. *Cape Fear* – North Carolina

Disney Films

Disney films are not just for children, they are a favourite of adults too and bring back fond memories. Test your memory with these questions.

1. In what decade was *Snow White* first released?
2. Who is the only actress to have won a Best Actress Oscar in a Disney film?
3. *The Jungle Book* was inspired by a book of the same name written by whom?
4. In what year did The Walt Disney Company acquire Lucasfilm?
5. Who plays the two main characters in *The Parent Trap* from 1961?
6. What is the real name of *Sleeping Beauty*?
7. Which Disney soundtrack includes Be Prepared, I Just Can't Wait to Be King and Hakuna Matata?
8. What was the title of the follow-up film to *Finding Nemo*?
9. Which Disney film features the voices of Miley Cyrus, John Travolta and Malcolm McDowell?
10. Which character sings Let It Go in the film *Frozen*?
11. Which Disney film is considered to be the most expensive animated movie ever made?
12. Who played Walt Disney in the film *Saving Mr Banks*?

Answers – Disney Films

1. 1930s
2. Julie Andrews in *Mary Poppins*
3. Rudyard Kipling
4. 2012 for over $4bn!
5. Hayley Mills, and her real dad played their dad!
6. Princess Aurora
7. *The Lion King*
8. *Finding Dory*
9. *Bolt*
10. Elsa
11. *Tangled*
12. Tom Hanks

Sci-fi Films

A great genre of films, give these Sci-Fi classics a try.

1. In the 1986 children's classic *Flight of the Navigator*, how many years into the future does young boy David Freeman travel?
2. Who starred alongside Roddy McDowall in the 1968 original of *Planet of the Apes*?
3. Who directed the 2014 blockbuster *Interstellar*?
4. What 1999 sci-fi hit, the first in a trilogy, was directed by the Wachowski Brothers/ Sisters?
5. What is the subtitle of the third Mad Max film, which was released in 1985?
6. In what decade was *Barbarella* released?
7. In what film did Arnold Schwarzenegger go for a virtual vacation to Mars?
8. In what 2009 film does a paraplegic marine get dispatched to the moon Pandora on a unique mission?
9. What 1927 film directed by Fritz Lang is considered a pioneering work of science fiction cinema?
10. What character was played by Harrison Ford in the 1982 film *Blade Runner*?
11. In *Men in Black*, according to the tagline, what are Will Smith and his colleagues protecting the Earth from?
12. In what film did Klaatu and Gort visit?

Answers – Sci-fi Films

1. 8 years (from 1978 to 1986)
2. Charlton Heston
3. Christopher Nolan
4. *The Matrix*. They are now sisters (they are both trans-women).
5. *Beyond Thunderdome*
6. The 1960s (1968)
7. *Total Recall*
8. *Avatar*
9. *Metropolis*
10. Rick Deckard
11. The scum of the universe.
12. *The Day the Earth Stood Still* (1951 and also 2008). Klaatu was a humanoid visitor, and Gort was his 8 foot tall robot.

2000s Films

Another decades quiz, this time from 2000-2009

1. What is the name of Robin William's character in *Night at the Museum*?
2. What language was *Crouching Tiger, Hidden Dragon* originally filmed in?
3. *Angels and Demons* was the sequel to which popular action film?
4. Who composed the musical soundtrack for 2000 film *Gladiator* earning him an Academy Award for Original Score?
5. What year was *The Island* released, 2001, 2005 or 2009?
6. *American Psycho* was adapted from a 1991 novel by which author?
7. *Ice Age* was released in 2002 by which studio?
8. In *Battle Royale*, which student will win the battle according to the rules?
9. Who plays central character John Anderton in film *Minority Report*?
10. In *Little Miss Sunshine*, which song does Olive dance to at her pageant?
11. Which Mancunian directed *28 Days Later*?
12. Will Smith plays an alcoholic with superpowers such as flight and superhuman strength in which 2008 film?

Answers – 2000s Films

1. Theodore Roosevelt
2. Chinese
3. *The Da Vinci Code*
4. Hans Zimmer
5. 2005
6. Bret Easton Ellis
7. 20th Century Fox
8. The last one alive (last man standing)
9. Tom Cruise
10. Superfreak
11. Danny Boyle
12. *Hancock*

Cities on Film

Which cities are these brilliant films set in?

1. *Amelie*
2. *L.A. Confidential*
3. *The Departed*
4. *Lost in Translation*
5. *Vertigo*
6. *The Girl with the Dragon Tattoo*
7. *The Sound of Music*
8. *A Room with a View*
9. *The Third Man*
10. *La Dolce Vita*
11. *Alfie*
12. *City of God*
13. *Educating Rita*
14. *Slumdog Millionaire*
15. *Once*

Answers – Cities on Film

1. *Amelie* - Paris
2. *L.A. Confidential* – Los Angeles
3. *The Departed* - Boston
4. *Lost in Translation* - Tokyo
5. *Vertigo* – San Francisco
6. *The Girl with the Dragon Tattoo* - Stockholm
7. *The Sound of Music* - Saltzburg
8. *A Room with a View* - Florence
9. *The Third Man* - Vienna
10. *La Dolce Vita* - Rome
11. *Alfie* - London
12. *City of God* – Rio de Janeiro
13. *Educating Rita* - Liverpool
14. *Slumdog Millionaire* - Mumbai
15. *Once* - Dublin

Children's Films

We say children's films, I mean some of these are super popular with adults too!

1. Name the yellow creatures in *Despicable Me*
2. Made into no fewer than 5 films is this story about an orphaned girl who lives in the Swiss Alps with her goat-herding grandfather. What is it called?
3. Which Japanese animation film studio's films includes *Spirited Away* and *Howl's Moving Castle*?
4. What three word phrase is repeatedly said by character Westley to Buttercup in *The Princess Bride?*
5. In the *Harry Potter* series of films who is the only Weasley daughter?
6. Which 1995 film has the tagline 'Roll the dice and release the excitement!'
7. Name the two children in *Chitty Chitty Bang Bang.*
8. Who appeared in over 30 films as a child, sang On the Good Ship Lollipop and died in 2014?
9. How old is Padme Amidala in *Star Wars: The Phantom Menace*?
10. Chunk, Stef, Mikey, One Eyed Willie and Fratelli appear in which film?
11. Who directed *The Nightmare Before Christmas*?
12. The 1996 film *Matilda* is based on a book by which children's author?

Answers – Children's Films

1. The Minions
2. *Heidi*
3. Studio Ghibli
4. As you wish
5. Ginny Weasley
6. *Jumanji*
7. Jeremy and Jemima
8. Shirley Temple
9. 14 years old
10. *The Goonies*
11. Tim Burton
12. Roald Dahl

1990s films

Another decades quiz spanning 1990 to 1999.

1. What black and white 1994 film, is about the life of two shop assistants over the course of a single day?
2. What Sofia Coppola directed film from 1999 was based on the bestselling book by Jeffrey Eugenides?
3. Which 1994 film has the tagline "Fear can hold you prisoner. Hope can set you free."?
4. Which actor starred alongside Michelle Pfeiffer in a C19th century tale of New York high society?
5. Which actor, later from *The West Wing*, played a sleazy corporate producer in *Wayne's World*?
6. What 1996 film featured Courtney Cox as a nosy newscaster, and David Arquette as a fumbling cop?
7. Who were Kevin Pollack, Benicio Del Toro, Stephen Baldwin, Gabriel Byrne and Kevin Spacey collectively known as?
8. What Shakespeare characters did Claire Danes play in the 1996 film directed by Baz Luhrmann?
9. What 1999 comedy featured the character James Emmanuel Levenstein?
10. Who plays Frank Bannister, in a 1996 film of a man who speaks to ghost and uses it to con people?
11. What colour card does Gerard Depardieu get with Andie MacDowell in the 1990 romantic comedy?
12. What is the first rule of *Fight Club?*

Answers – 1990s films

1. *Clerks*
2. *The Virgin Suicides*
3. *The Shawshank Redemption*
4. Daniel Day Lewis in *The Age of Innocence*
5. Rob Lowe
6. *Scream*
7. *The Usual Suspects*
8. Juliet
9. *American Pie* - he was known in the film as Jim
10. Michael J Fox, in *The Frighteners*
11. Green. The film is *Green Card*, and the two get married so Depardieu can get a Green Card and the right to live and work in the US
12. You don't talk about Fight Club

Film Star Clues

Can you figure out the film star these clues are about? Start with no. 1 and work your way down, the fewer clues you need the better!

1. I am male
2. I've been known to get easily annoyed
3. I am an American
4. I was born in 1937
5. My debut film was *The Cry Baby Killer* in 1958.
6. I have been nominated for an Oscar in five successive decades
7. I used to be a messenger boy for MGM's cartoon department
8. I used to have a very big smile
9. I played Frank Costello in *The Departed*
10. I was asked to play the role of Michael Corleone in *The Godfather*
11. I once played the character Colonel Nathan R Jessop
12. I appeared in *The Shining*
13. My initials are J.N.
14. I won a Best Actor Oscar for *As Good as it Gets*
15. I played The Joker in the 1989 film *Batman*

Answers – Film Star Clues

Answer: Jack Nicholson

Superheroes

How many questions can you get right in this super quiz?

1. How many *Superman* films did Christopher Reeve appear in?
2. What character did Patrick Stewart play in the *X-Men* films?
3. What superhero is played by Gal Gadot?
4. Which 2009 superhero film was based on a comic book series written by Alan Moore?
5. Bryan Singer directed *Superman Returns*, but is best known for which superhero movie series?
6. What group were Blue Raja, Shoveler and Furious a part of?
7. Ben Affleck has played *Batman* and which other superhero?
8. In what superhero film does a football player and his friends travel to the planet Mongo?
9. Which comedy actor played The Riddler in 1995 film *Batman Forever*?
10. Which superheroes are named after painters, mainly from the Renaissance period?

Answers – Superheroes

1. 4 – *Superman I, II, III, IV*, between 1978 and 1987. He also appeared in the Smallville TV series between 2003 and 2004.
2. Professor Charles Xavier
3. *Wonder Woman*
4. Watchmen
5. The *X-Men films*
6. *The Mystery Men*
7. Daredevil
8. *Flash Gordon*
9. Jim Carrey
10. The Teenage Mutant Ninja Turtles

Animals on Film

These directors obviously didn't hear the phrase never work with animals or children!

1. What is the name of Dr Evil's cat in the *Austin Powers* series of films?
2. How did they get the DNA to clone the dinosaurs in *Jurassic Park*?
3. What breed of dog is Scooby Doo?
4. Who is the animal star of the film *Ratatouille*?
5. A 1963 American film starring David Niven and Peter Cushing about a huge diamond named what?
6. Elizabeth Taylor's spellbinding portrayal in the 1960s, saw Cleopatra killed by which animal?
7. *Animal House* is a film in which genre?
8. In *The Omen*, what kind of animals attack Damien's car in the safari park?
9. The 2016 film *Nocturnal Animal* was nominated for nine BAFTAs, including one for Best Actor in a Leading Role for which American actor?
10. Diane Fossey, primatologist and conservationist was portrayed by Sigourney Weaver in which 1988 film?
11. Natalie Portman received her first (and only as of 2017) Best Actress Oscar, for which animal related film of 2010?
12. The first ever Lassie film had what title?

Answers – Animals on Film

1. Mr Bigglesworth
2. From insects preserved in amber/ tree resin (the insects had fed on dinosaur blood)
3. A Great Dane
4. A rat chef called Remy
5. The Pink Panther
6. An asp-a kind of snake
7. Comedy – it is a National Lampoons film
8. Baboons
9. Jake Gyllenhaal
10. *Gorillas in the Mist*
11. *Black Swan*
12. *Lassie Come Home*

Harrison Ford Films

An actor of the first-class order, see if you can remember all his acting credits!

1. In what film does Harrison Ford go into hiding in Amish country to protect a young boy?
2. In what year was he born, 1942, 1947 or 1952?
3. Which actress became Ford's 3rd wife in 2010?
4. In what 1967 Western was his first credited film role?
5. What iconic character does he play in the Star Wars films?
6. In what 1973 George Lucas film did he play the character of Bob Falfa?
7. In what two films did he play Tom Clancy's spy, Jack Ryan?
8. What rock band was he a stagehand for in the 1970s?
9. In what film did he play fictional US President James Marshall?
10. In what film did he play multi-millionaire businessman Linus Larrabee?
11. In the 1993 film *The Fugitive*, why was he on the run?
12. Harrison Ford stars as Rick Deckard in the sci-fi classic *Blade Runner*. It was released in 1982, but in what year was it set?

Answers - Harrison Ford Films

1. *Witness*
2. 1942
3. Calista Flockhart
4. *A Time for Killing*
5. Han Solo
6. *American Graffitti*
7. *Clear and Present Danger* and *Patriot Games*
8. *The Doors*
9. *Air Force One*
10. *Sabrina*
11. He was unjustly accused of murdering his wife
12. 2019

Film descriptions

Can you identify the following films from these brief descriptions?

1. A bullied teenage girl exacts revenge on her tormentors after developing telekinetic powers.
2. Sweethearts Brad and Janet get a flat tyre in a storm and discover the eerie mansion of a mad scientist.
3. After getting a Green Card in exchange for assassinating a Cuban official, Tony Montana stakes a claim on the Miami drug trade.
4. Two detectives pursue a serial killer who targets people he thinks represent the seven deadly sins.
5. All he ever wanted was to be a professional hockey player, but he instead joins a golf tournament to try and stop his grandmother from losing her home.
6. In a post-apocalyptic future, a nomadic traveller delivers mail – and hope – to north-west America.
7. Henry discovers his ex-girlfriend is pregnant but the baby turns out to be a bizarre lizard creature.
8. A pregnant police chief investigates homicides after a man hires criminals to kidnap his wife.
9. Johnny Rico is doing military service in the Mobile Infantry in an interstellar war against the "Bugs".
10. Secretary Marion Crane stays at a secluded motel after she steals from her employer and discovers the motel's disturbed owner.

Answers – Film descriptions

1. *Carrie*
2. *The Rocky Horror Picture Show*
3. *Scarface*
4. *Seven*
5. *Happy Gilmore*
6. *The Postman*
7. *Eraserhead*
8. *Fargo*
9. *Starship Troopers*
10. *Psycho*

1980s Films

A decades quiz for the 1980s this time. Test your knowledge of 1980 to 1989.

1. What club were Brat Pack stars Emilio Estevez, Judd Nelson, Molly Ringwald and Ally Sheedy in, in the 1985 John Hughes film?
2. What exactly were the *Lost Boys* in the 1987 film?
3. In what 1988 film did Christian Slater and Winona Ryder play teenage killers?
4. Which 1980 film directed by Martin Scorsese led to an Academy Award and a Golden Globe for the leading actor?
5. Everyone knows that Arnie played the *Terminator* in the 1984 sci-fi classic, but who did Linda Hamilton play?
6. In what 1984 film was a demi-god called Zuul found in a refrigerator?
7. What was the highest grossing film of the 1980s?
8. Which cheeky Detroit detective did Eddie Murphy play in the 1984 film *Beverly Hills Cop?*
9. In the 1985 classic film *Top Gun,* Tom Cruise was "Maverick", but who was Val Kilmer?
10. What eponymous high-tech superhero is played by Peter Weller in the 1987 film?

Answers - 1980s films

1. *The Breakfast Club*
2. Vampires
3. *Heathers*
4. *Raging Bull*
5. Sarah Connor
6. *Ghostbusters*
7. *E.T the Extra-Terrestrial*
8. Axel Foley
9. Iceman
10. *Robocop*

Film Anagrams

We have mixed up the names of some well-known films – see if you can rearrange them to find the answers.

1. Wacko Groan Locker (1971)
2. Europe Shiftmen (1987)
3. Area Pits (2019)
4. Reptile Togs (1982)
5. Maniac Tea Buyer (1999)
6. So Twisty Deers (1961)
7. Very Pining Avatars (1998)
8. Tainting Sport (1996)
9. Canoodle Hulk (1967)
10. Mint Fetish Vengeance (1960)

Answers – Film Anagrams

1. *A Clockwork Orange*
2. *Empire of the Sun*
3. *Parasite*
4. *Poltergeist*
5. *American Beauty*
6. *West Side Story*
7. *Saving Private Ryan*
8. *Trainspotting*
9. *Cool Hand Luke*
10. *The Magnificent Seven*

Guess the Film

Can you figure out the film these clues are about? Start with no. 1 and work your way down, the fewer clues you need the better!

1. This is a comedy
2. Electricity features heavily in this film
3. The film spawned two sequels
4. The studio executive in charge of the film wanted to call it 'Spaceman from Pluto'
5. The film only won one Oscar, for best sound effects editing.
6. This is a science fiction film
7. Eric Stoltz was originally due to star in the lead role
8. Bob Gale was one of the co-writers of the film
9. Crispin Glover played a young dad
10. Huey Lewis and the News sang the main theme song.
11. The film was set in Hill Valley, California.
12. One of the main characters in the film liked to say, "Great Scott!"
13. The film was co-written and directed by Robert Zemeckis
14. This film starred Michael J Fox
15. 88mph is the speed you need to get to.

Answer – Guess the Film

This film is a favourite of ours, *Back to the Future*. Released in 1985, it features teenage American Marty McFly who travels back in time to 1955 and has to try and get his parents together after his mother accidentally falls in love with him. But then you probably knew that already, didn't you?

Romantic Comedies

What do remember about these fantastic rom coms?

1. What does Hugh Grant do for a living in the 1999 film, *Notting Hill*?
2. Who starred as "Bud" Baxter in the 1960 Billy Wilder directed film *The Apartment*?
3. Through what medium do main characters Sam Baldwin and Annie Reed meet in the 1993 hit film *Sleepless in Seattle*?
4. Who played Mary in *There's Something About Mary*?
5. *Before Sunrise* is about a young man and woman who meet on a train and spend one evening together, but in which city is it set?
6. *It Happened One Night* starred which actor as a reporter called Peter?
7. Which 1997 film has Julia Roberts trying to break off her friend's wedding with just a few days to go when she realises, she's in love with him?
8. Sandra Bullock is mistaken for the fiancée of a coma patient in which 1995 film?
9. In 2019 film Yesterday, musician Jack Malik is suddenly the only person who can remember the music of which group?
10. The original book is by JoJo Moyes and the 2016 film features Emilia Clarke – name the film?

Answers – Romantic Comedies

1. He is a bookshop owner
2. Jack Lemmon
3. Through a radio talk show, Sam phones up and Annie hears him and impulsively writes to him and asks to meet him at the Empire State Building on Valentine's Day
4. Cameron Diaz
5. Vienna
6. Clark Gable
7. *My Best Friend's Wedding*
8. *While You Were Sleeping*
9. The Beatles
10. *Me Before You*

1970s Films

This next decades quiz about the 1970s – test your knowledge from 1970 to 1979

1. Who played 'Little Big Man' in the 1970 film of the same name?
2. Which eponymous cool guy did Richard Rowntree play in 1971?
3. Jeff Bridges and Cybill Shepherd starred in which nostalgic Peter Bogdanovich film in 1971, based on a novel by Larry McMurty?
4. What was the occupation of Gene Hackman's character in *The Poseidon Adventure*?
5. Who directed the 1972 Oscar winning film *The Godfather*?
6. In the 1976 film *All the President's Men*, who is the President?
7. Which music legend starred in *The Man Who Fell to Earth*?
8. Who played the Bandit in *Smokey and the Bandit*?
9. Richard Dreyfuss played Elliot Garfield in which 1977 romantic drama?
10. In 1979 film *Hair*, which war is the main character intending to enlist in?
11. In what US state is *The Amityville Horror* set?
12. What year was *Bugsy Malone* released?

Answers – 1970s Films

1. Dustin Hoffman
2. Shaft
3. *The Last Picture Show*
4. Vicar
5. Francis Ford Coppola
6. Richard Nixon
7. David Bowie
8. Burt Reynolds
9. *The Goodbye Girl*
10. The Vietnam War
11. New York
12. 1976

Colours

All of these films have a colour in the title. Can you guess them?

1. Which 1980s film directed by David Lynch has the tagline 'It's a Strange World'?
2. Oprah Winfrey played Sofia in which colourful film?
3. Which 2002 film, a prequel to a 1991 film, featured the songs 'He's Back!' and 'Enter the Dragon'?
4. Which 1992 comedy film features Woody Harrelson and Wesley Snipes?
5. Which Mandarin film released in 2006 features Chow Yun-fat as the emperor? We're looking for the translation not the original Chinese title!
6. Which colourful Woody Allen film, starring Mia Farrow and Jeff Daniels, is set 1935 New Jersey?
7. Which classic monster horror film was novelised twice under the pseudonyms Vargo Statten and Carl Dreadstone?
8. Which 2011 American superhero film was directed by Martin Campbell?
9. Which musical Baz Luhrmann film includes a medley featuring a song by The Beatles, U2, David Bowie and Dolly Parton?
10. Which 1989 film stars Clint Eastwood with cameo appearances from Jim Carrey and Bryan Adams?

Answers – Colours

1. *Blue Velvet*
2. *The Color Purple*
3. *Red Dragon*
4. *White Men Can't Jump*
5. *Curse of the Golden Flower*
6. *The Purple Rose of Cairo*
7. *The Creature from the Black Lagoon*
8. *Green Lantern*
9. *Moulin Rouge*
10. *Pink Cadillac*

Number Films

All of these film titles contain a number…

1. 1999 mystery thriller directed by Joel Schumacher starring Nicholas Cage and Joaquin Phoenix
2. 2005 rom-com directed by Judd Apatow starring Steve Carell, Catherine Keener and Paul Rudd
3. 1987 comedy drama directed by Leonard Nimoy starring Tom Selleck, Ted Danson and Steve Guttenberg
4. 1970 war comedy drama directed by Mike Nichols starring Alan Arkin, Martin Balsam and Art Garfunkel
5. A pretty and popular teenager is told by her dad she can't go on a date until her older, uninterested sister does (1999)
6. A man becomes obsessed by a novel he believes was written about him (2007)
7. An old man is incarcerated for claiming he is the real Santa Claus. Cue a young lawyer and little girl to fight his corner (1947/ 1994)
8. Which film links Sigourney Weaver, Ridley Scott, Gerard Depardieu, Santa Maria and Vangellis
9. Which film links Stanley Kubrick, *The Sentinel*, 1968, Dr Heywood Floyd and Leonard Rossiter
10. Which film links Meat Loaf, Liverpool, Ronny Yu, 92 minutes, Elmo and Robert Carlyle?

Answers – Numbers Films

1. *8mm*
2. *The 40 Year Old Virgin*
3. *Three Men and a Baby*
4. *Catch 22*
5. *10 Things I Hate About You*
6. *The Number 23*
7. *Miracle on 34th Street*
8. *1492: Conquest of Paradise*
9. *2001: A Space Odyssey*
10. *51st State*

Real Star Names

These are their real names, but how are these actors and actresses better known to us

1. Mark Sinclair
2. Ilyena Lydia Vasilevna Mironov
3. Shelton Lee
4. Norma Jean Mortenson
5. Neta Lee Hershlag
6. Krishna Pandit Bhanji
7. Archibald Leach
8. Audrey Kathleen Ruston
9. Maurice Micklewhite
10. Michael Douglas (this isn't a trick question, the answer isn't Michael Douglas!)
11. Cornelius Crane Chase
12. Caryn Elaine Johnson
13. Eric Marlon Bishop
14. Chan Kong-sang
15. Issur Danielovitch

Answers - Real Star Names

1. Vin Diesel
2. Helen Mirren
3. Spike Lee
4. Marilyn Monroe
5. Natalie Portman
6. Sir Ben Kingsley
7. Cary Grant
8. Audrey Hepburn (she was the daughter of a Dutch nobleman)
9. Michael Caine
10. Michael Keaton
11. Chevy Chase
12. Whoopie Goldberg
13. Jamie Foxx
14. Jackie Chan
15. Kirk Douglas

Three English Dames

Judi Dench, Julie Walters and Maggie Smith are three of Britain's most acclaimed actresses and have all been made a Dame. But can you work out which Dame is in which film?

1. Mother Superior in *Sister Act*?
2. M in *Skyfall*?
3. Queen Elizabeth in *Shakespeare in Love*?
4. Aunt Ruth in *A Boy Called Christmas*?
5. Mrs Bird in *Paddington*?
6. Arabella in *Tea with Mussolini*?
7. Molly Weasley in the Harry Potter films?
8. Jean Brodie in *The Prime of Miss Jean Brodie*?
9. Philomena Lee in *Philomena*?
10. Rosie in *Mamma Mia*?
11. Annie in *Calendar Girls*?
12. Old Deuteronomy in *Cats*?
13. Janet in *Ladies in Lavender*?
14. Mrs Wilkinson in *Billy Elliot*?
15. Granny Wendy in *Hook*?

Answers - Three English Dames

1. Maggie Smith
2. Judi Dench
3. Judi Dench
4. Maggie Smith
5. Julie Walters
6. Judi Dench
7. Julie Walters
8. Maggie Smith
9. Judi Dench
10. Julie Walters
11. Julie Walters
12. Judi Dench
13. Maggie Smith
14. Julie Walters
15. Maggie Smith

1960s Films

Head down memory lane to the 1960s

1. Which film won an Academy Award for Best Score and included songs 'Who Will Buy', 'Boy for Sale' and 'Oom Pah-Pah'?
2. What year was *Zulu* released with Michael Caine?
3. What rating was film *Lolita* originally given at its cinema release?
4. Who played Holly Golightly's love interest Paul Varjak in *Breakfast at Tiffany's*?
5. Who directed *Lawrence of Arabia*? He also directed *Brief Encounter* and *Bridge on the River Kwai*.
6. Who was fired from the cast of *Valley of the Dolls* due to her drinking and behaviour?
7. What year did *Midnight Cowboy* win the Academy Award for Best Picture?
8. *My Fair Lady* was based on which stage play by George Bernard Shaw?
9. *The Great Escape* centres around a group of prisoners during which world war?
10. Who is the main character yet plays 'a man with no name' in *A Fistful of Dollars*?
11. Who directed *Spartacus*? He is considered one of the best directors of all time and died in 1999.
12. Which 1963 film's lead actress signed on for a record-setting guaranteed million-dollar salary?

Answers- 1960s Films

1. *Oliver!*
2. 1964
3. An X rating meaning no one under 18 years could see it
4. George Peppard
5. David Lean
6. Judy Garland
7. 1969
8. *Pygmalion*
9. World War II
10. Clint Eastwood
11. Stanley Kubrick
12. *Cleopatra* – for Elizabeth Taylor

Missing Vowels

Can you identify these film titles – they are in plain sight, just with the vowels removed. Also they have all been nominated for a Best Picture Oscar, but none actually won. As an extra clue, I've given the year of the Oscars in brackets.

1. FV SY PCS (1970)
2. DG DY FTRNN (1975)
3. DD PTS SCTY (1989)
4. SHN (1996)
5. SBSCT (2003)
6. CRLN (2009)
7. RM (2015)
8. SNGNG _N TE RN (1952)
9. MLFCNT (2014)
10. BG TRBL _N LTTL CHN (1986)
11. KND HRTS _ND CRNTS (1949)
12. TH CRW (1994)

Answers - Missing Vowels

1. *Five Easy Pieces*
2. *Dog Day Afternoon*
3. *Dead Poet's Society*
4. *Shine*
5. *Seabiscuit*
6. *Coraline*
7. *Room*
8. *Singing in the Rain*
9. *Maleficent*
10. *Big Trouble in Little China*
11. *Kind Hearts and Coronets*
12. *The Crow*

Harry Potter

How could we do a quiz without a round on perennial favourite Harry Potter?

1. Who gives Harry Potter the gift of his owl Hedwig?
2. Who plays the Defence Against the Dark Teacher in *Harry Potter and the Chamber of Secrets*?
3. Where does Harry first open the dragon's egg in *Harry Potter and the Goblet of Fire*?
4. The tagline 'The Rebellion Begins' is from which film?
5. Which teacher warns Harry of 'The Grim' in his tea leaves?
6. Which Hogwarts house is blue in colour?
7. What is the address of Sirius Black's house and ancestral home?
8. How many balls are there in Quidditch?
9. What are names of Ron's parents?
10. How many Harry Potter films did Chris Columbus direct?
11. Who plays wandmaker Ollivander in the Harry Potter films?
12. What poisons Ron in *Harry Potter and the Half Blood Prince*?

Answers – Harry Potter

1. Hagrid
2. Kenneth Branagh
3. The Gryffindor common room
4. *Harry Potter and the Order of the Phoenix*
5. Professor Sybill Trelawny
6. Ravenclaw
7. 12 Grimmauld Place
8. Four – one snitch, one quaffle and two bludgers
9. Molly and Arthur Weasley
10. Two
11. John Hurt
12. Oak-matured mead meant for Albus Dumbledore

More Anagrams

Another set of anagrams to wake up your brain!

1. Is Hen Night (1980)
2. Lo Lowly Sheep (1999)
3. Oust Kevin (2019)
4. Farmer Snorts (2007)
5. Hen Rub (1959)
6. Whole Lane (1978)
7. Nina Arm (1988)
8. Cane No Sleeve (2001)
9. Gong Kink (1933)
10. Ana Quam (2018)

Answers - More Anagrams

1. *The Shining*
2. *Sleepy Hollow*
3. *Knives Out*
4. *Transformers*
5. *Ben Hur*
6. *Halloween*
7. *Rain Man*
8. *Ocean's Eleven*
9. *King Kong*
10. *Aquaman*

A Bit of a Mix

A mixed bag of questions to tempt you

1. Which 1997 film features Judi Dench as Queen Victoria?
2. Mulan pretends to be a man and takes her father's place to fight against whom?
3. *How Green Was My Valley* is set in which part of the world?
4. "Skip to My Lou", "The Trolley Song" and "Have Yourself a Merry Little Christmas" are all songs from which 1944 MGM film?
5. In the 2005 film *Manderlay* Danish director Lars Von Trier had the cast kill which animal for food during filming? It was reported that actor John C Reilly dropped out of the film due to this.
6. How many more Dalmatians are there in the sequel, according to the film from 2000, than the original?
7. *Life of Pi* is a film from 2012 that see an Indian teenager adrift on the ocean with a tiger. Who wrote the original novel?
8. In the film *Annie* from 1982, who takes Annie on as his ward?
9. In the 1957 film *Old Yeller*, what is Old Yeller?
10. Who was the voice of Woody in the 1995 film, *Toy Story*?

Answers – A Bit of a Mix

1. Mrs Brown
2. The Huns
3. Wales
4. *Meet Me in St Louis*
5. A donkey – the scenes were meant to be in the film but after the intervention of animal rights campaigners it was removed.
6. One – the original is *101 Dalmatians* and the sequel is *102 Dalmatians*
7. Yann Martel
8. Oliver Warbucks
9. A dog
10. Tom Hanks

More Film Descriptions

A few more descriptions of some great films – can you get them from their short description?

1. In a small town, 3 men prepare for marriage and military service, by going on one last hunting trip.
2. In a dystopian 1988, a prisoner is given 24 hours to rescue the President of the USA for a pardon.
3. A small-town boxer from working class Philadelphia is arbitrarily chosen to take on the reigning world heavyweight champion.
4. A reluctant dwarf must play a critical role in protecting a special baby from an evil queen.
5. A young blonde-haired girl has adventures with twins, a colourful cat and a red queen.
6. A terrorist has taken a bus hostage and it is vital the bus does not stop or it will blow up!
7. An old balloon salesman, Carl, is ready to fulfil his lifelong dream but finds a stowaway called Russell.
8. An undercover FBI agent must find out who wants to sabotage the Miss United States Pageant by going to extreme lengths.
9. A prisoner is mentored by his cellmate and after his release while looking for a club singing job, meets a music promoter and becomes a star.
10. A German industrialist saves Jewish people in WW2 by employing them in his factories.

Answers – More Film Descriptions

1. *The Deer Hunter*
2. *Escape From New York*
3. *Rocky*
4. *Willow*
5. *Alice in Wonderland*
6. *Speed*
7. *Up*
8. *Miss Congeniality*
9. *Jailhouse Rock*
10. *Schindler's List*

1950s Films

The 1950s are upon us! Here are the set for 1950 to 1959.

1. In the popular musical, how many brides are there for the seven brothers?
2. Who starred as the Princess alongside Gregory Peck in 1953 film *Roman Holiday*?
3. *The King & I* is about an English tutor working for the King of which Asian country?
4. In *12 Angry Men*, what are the twelve men collectively known as?
5. The 1956 film *High Society* was the last professional film role of which starlet who later became Princess of Monaco?
6. Was *Carry on Sergeant* the 1st or 2nd Carry on Film?
7. Who turned down the lead role in *High Noon* saying he hated it and it was "un-American"?
8. *Hobson's Choice* was released in 1951, 1954 or 1957?
9. *A Streetcar Named Desire* won three Academy Awards – name one.
10. Who directed the musical *An American in Paris*? He arguably had a wife more famous than him.
11. A black and white film featuring Jack Lemmon, Tony Curtis and Marilyn Monroe. Name the film?
12. *Peter Pan*, the 1953 film by Walt Disney Productions was adapted from a book by which author?

Answers - 1950s Films

1. Seven
2. Audrey Hepburn
3. Siam/ Thailand
4. The Jury/ Jurors
5. Grace Kelly
6. First
7. John Wayne
8. 1954
9. Best Actress in a Leading Role, Best Actress in a Supporting Role and Best Supporting Actor
10. Vincente Minelli (husband of Judy Garland)
11. *Some Like it Hot*
12. J M Barrie

Morgan Freeman

The legend that is Morgan Freeman, but how much do you know about him?

1. Morgan Freeman has only won one Academy Award despite many nominations – for which film of 2004?
2. He has also only won one Golden Globe – for which film?
3. Which character does he play in *Bruce Almighty*?
4. Which actor directed Morgan Freeman in *Gone Baby Gone* – it was his feature-length directorial debut?
5. What was his only film of 2010 starring alongside Helen Mirren, Bruce Willis and John Malkovich?
6. What is the name of his character in *The Dark Knight* Trilogy?
7. His 2003 film *Dreamcatcher* is adapted from a novel by which author?
8. In *Robin Hood Prince of Thieves*, he plays Azeem, but who plays Robin?
9. In *Along Came a Spider* and *Kiss the Girls*, what is the name of his character, penned by thriller writer James Patterson?
10. In what magical 2013 film did he first play Thaddeus Bradley?

Answers - Morgan Freeman

1. *Million Dollar Baby*
2. *Driving Miss Daisy*
3. God
4. Ben Affleck
5. *Red*
6. Lucius Fox
7. Stephen King
8. Kevin Costner
9. Alex Cross
10. *Now You See Me*

Marvel Actors

Can you name the actor for each of these Marvel characters? We've added a film they featured in.

1. Nick Fury in *Spider-Man Far from Home*
2. Carol Danvers/ Captain Marvel in *Captain Marvel*
3. Doctor Stephen Strange in *Doctor Strange*
4. Groot (Voice) in *Guardians of the Galaxy*
5. Heimdall in *Thor*
6. Thanos in *Avengers: Infinity War*
7. Tony Stark / Iron Man in *Iron Man*
8. Wong in *Shang-Chi and the Legend of the Ten Rings*
9. Natasha Romanoff / Black Widow in *Black Widow*
10. Steve Rogers/ Captain America in *Captain America: The First Avenger*
11. Loki in *Thor Ragnarok*
12. Pepper Potts in *Iron Man 2*
13. Wanda Maximoff / Scarlet Witch in *The Avengers: Age of Ultron*
14. J.A.R.V.I.S. in *The Avengers*
15. Nebula in *Guardians of the Galaxy Vol.2*

Answers – Marvel Actors

1. Samuel L Jackson
2. Brie Larson
3. Benedict Cumberbatch
4. Vin Diesel
5. Idris Elba
6. Josh Brolin
7. Robert Downey Jr.
8. Benedict Wong
9. Scarlett Johansson
10. Chris Evans
11. Tom Hiddleston
12. Gwyneth Paltrow
13. Elizabeth Olsen
14. Paul Bettany
15. Karen Gillan

Gone Too Soon

Here are some clues to actors and actresses who sadly died young. Can you figure out who they are?

1. Born 18th August 1952 in Houston, Texas; he played a dead man opposite Demi Moore; he was married to Lisa Niemi after his mum taught her to dance.
2. He died in 2020; his last film was *Ma Rainey's Black Bottom*; he studied directing at Howard University.
3. Her breakthrough role was in *Clueless*; she died aged 32; her husband was Simon Monjack
4. He played the lead role in *Capote*; he was born and died in New York; his stage name is three names
5. She had three husbands; she was in *The Misfits*; she died in 1962
6. He is best known as a comedy actor; his first film role was in *Popeye* (1980); he called his children Zelda, Zachary and Cody
7. He was in a few films including *East of Eden* and *Giant;* he had a car crash; he was born in 1931
8. She was married to Liam Neeson; she died while skiing; she was in *Nell* and *The White Countess*
9. He was filming *The Imaginarium of Doctor Parnassus* when he died; he was Australian and in 20 films
10. She received an Academy Award nomination for *Rebel Without a Cause*; her daughter is actress Natasha Gregson Wagner; she sang in film *Gypsy*

Answers- Gone Too Soon

1. Patrick Swayze
2. Chadwick Boseman
3. Brittany Murphy
4. Philip Seymour Hoffman
5. Marilyn Monroe
6. Robin Williams
7. James Dean
8. Natasha Richardson
9. Heath Ledger
10. Natalie Wood

More of a Mix

Another mix of questions to enjoy

1. Who directed the 1993 film Groundhog Day?
2. Who played Tommy DeVito in the 1990 film *Goodfellas*?
3. The 1997 film *Contact* starring Jodie Foster was based on a novel by which famous scientist?
4. Which actor got his breakthrough leading role in the 2000 film *Pitch Black*?
5. Which 2000 sci-fi film starring Dennis Quaid and Jim Caviezel was remade as a TV series in 2016?
6. Which Scottish actress voiced Merida in *Brave*?
7. What is the name of the 2019 biopic about Elton John?
8. What is the name of Pinocchio's father?
9. Which film stars Matt Damon, Robin Williams, Ben Affleck and Minnie Driver?
10. The popular 2021 Chinese War film is titled The Battle at Lake _____ what?

Answers - More of a Mix

1. Harold Ramis
2. Joe Pesci
3. Carl Sagan
4. Vin Diesel
5. Frequency
6. Kelly MacDonald
7. *Rocketman*
8. Geppetto
9. *Good Will Hunting*
10. Changjin

Real or Fake

Below are some film titles. Some are real (honest) and some are fake - which is which?

1. *tick, tick…Boom!*
2. *Santa with Muscles*
3. *Black Sheep Squadron*
4. *Time to Sleep*
5. *One Night in Seattle*
6. *Generation XYZ*
7. *Dramatic Mother*
8. *Gun Crazy*
9. *Quackser Fortune Has a Cousin in the Bronx*
10. *Treeman Duke*
11. *Stop! Or My Mom Will Shoot*
12. *Mr. Bruce*
13. *The Bye Bye Man*
14. *End of the Vampire King*
15. *Attack of the Killer Tomatoes!*

Answers – Real or Fake

1. Real – 2021 film
2. Real – 1996 film
3. Real – 1976 film
4. Fake
5. Real – 2013 film
6. Fake
7. Fake
8. Real – 1950 film
9. Real – 1970 film
10. Fake
11. Real – 1992 film
12. Fake
13. Real -2017 film
14. Fake
15. Real – 1978 film

A Trio of Characters

Here are names of three characters- can you say what film do they appear in?

1. Mildred Hayes, Bill Willoughby, Sam Rockwell (2017)
2. Augustus Gloop, Grandpa Joe, Mike Tevee (1971)
3. Richard Williams, Serena Williams, Oracene 'Brandy' Price (2021)
4. Benedick, Beatrice, Hero (1993)
5. Fantine, Cosette, Jean Valjean (2012)
6. Moses, Rameses, Nefretiri (1956)
7. Sherlock Holmes, Lestrade, Tewkesbury (2020)
8. Rosemary Woodhouse, Dr. Sapirstein, Hutch (1968)
9. Nancy Thompson, Tina Gray, Freddie Krueger (1984)
10. Queen Anne, Abigail Masham, Sarah Churchill (2018)

Answers – A Trio of Characters

1. *Three Billboards Outside Ebbing, Missouri*
2. *Willy Wonka and the Chocolate Factory*
3. *King Richard*
4. *Much Ado About Nothing*
5. *Les Miserables*
6. *The Ten Commandments*
7. *Enola Holmes*
8. *Rosemary's Baby*
9. *A Nightmare on Elm Street*
10. *The Favourite*

1930s & 1940s Films

Our last foray into the decades from 1930 - 1949

1. Who famously played *Frankenstein* in the 1931 film?
2. Which actor starred in *City Lights* and *Modern Times* in the 1930s, and died on Christmas Day 1977?
3. What is the surname of the four brothers who appeared in 1933 film *Duck Soup*?
4. Who directed the 1935 film *The Thirty Nine Steps*?
5. The film *The Invisible Man* of 1933 was an adaptation of a book of the same name – who was it written by?
6. The 1938 film *The Adventures of Robin Hood* and the 1940 film *Rebecca* both had outstanding leading ladies but how were they related?
7. Who wrote the screenplay, produced, directed and starred in *Citizen Kane*?
8. *Fantasia* featured which famous cartoon character?
9. In the 1941 film The *Maltese Falcon*, main character Sam Spade had which job?
10. Which author wrote the screenplay for *The Third Man* and later went on to be nominated for the Nobel Prize for Literature in 1966 and 1967?
11. *Gone With the Wind* takes place during which war?
12. *Mr Smith Goes to Washington* was created by which production company? Founded in 1918, renamed in 1924 it is one of the biggest in the world today.

Answers – 1930s & 1940s films

1. Boris Karloff
2. Sir Charlie Chaplin
3. The Marx brothers – Groucho, Harpo, Chico and Zeppo (fifth brother Gummo was not in this film)
4. Alfred Hitchcock
5. H.G.Wells
6. They were sisters- Olivia de Havilland and Joan Fontaine
7. Orson Wells
8. Mickey Mouse
9. A private detective
10. Graham Greene
11. The American Civil War
12. Columbia Pictures

More Film Star Clues

Can you figure out the film star these clues are about? Start with no. 1 and work your way down, the fewer clues you need the better.

1. I was born in 1969
2. My middle name is Lynn
3. I have played a stripper
4. I was born in New York
5. I have had three husbands
6. I was in *Anaconda*
7. I once said Madonna was my first big musical influence
8. My latest film is *Marry Me* (2022)
9. I sang on several charitable singles
10. I played opposite Ralph Fiennes in *Maid in Manhattan*
11. I was the first Latin actress to earn over $1 million for a film
12. I have dated Ben Affleck
13. I played the lead role in *The Wedding Planner*
14. I am best known by a three letter name
15. I am best known as a singer

Answer- More Film Star Clues

Answer - Jennifer Lopez

Taglines

These are the taglines to some famous films – can you guess them from their tagline alone?

1. A comedy about growing up…and the bumps along the way (2007)
2. From the moment they met it was murder (1944)
3. They're young, they're in love, and they kill people (1967)
4. For Harry and Lloyd, every day is a no-brainer (1994)
5. Escape or die frying (2000)
6. Man is the warmest place to hide (1982)
7. Nice planet. We'll take it (1996)
8. You will orbit into the fantastic future (1960)
9. We scare because we care (2001)
10. The first casualty of war is innocence (1986)
11. Houston, we have a problem (1995)
12. Surviving America in the twenty-first century (2020)
13. When he pours, he reigns (1988)
14. Makes Ben Hur look epic (1975)
15. Love never dies (1992)

Answers – Taglines

1. *Juno*
2. *Double Indemnity*
3. *Bonnie and Clyde*
4. *Dumb and Dumber*
5. *Chicken Run*
6. *The Thing*
7. *Mars Attacks!*
8. *The Time Machine*
9. *Monsters Inc.*
10. *Platoon*
11. *Apollo 13*
12. *Nomadland*
13. *Cocktail*
14. *Monty Python and the Holy Grail*
15. *Bram Stoker's Dracula*

Title Translations

These film titles were translated from English into another language for a different audience, and then translated back again. We have given you the new English translation and the country it received its odd translation. Can you work out which famous film it is meant to be?

1. Six Naked Pigs (China)
2. Vaseline (Venezuela)
3. Warm Shots (Czech Republic)
4. The Gun Died Laughing (Israel)
5. I'm Drunk and You're a Prostitute (Japan)
6. Full of the Nuts (Germany)
7. Pigs and Diamonds (Mexico)
8. Odd Couple, Wacky Trip, Go Together in Time for Birth (Thailand)
9. The Teeth from The Sea (France)
10. Please Do Not Touch the Old Women (Italy)
11. American Virgin Man (China)
12. Cat, Don't Touch His Hat! (Croatia)

Answers – Title Translations

1. The Full Monty
2. Grease
3. Hot Shots
4. The Naked Gun
5. Leaving Las Vegas
6. Dodgeball
7. Snatch
8. Due Date
9. Jaws
10. The Producers
11. American Pie
12. The Cat in the Hat

Chicken or Egg

What came first, the chicken or the egg….or basically just which of these two films?

1. *Who Framed Roger Rabbit* or *Dune*?
2. *The King's Speech* or *The Book Thief*?
3. *The Towering Inferno* or *The Zodiac Killer*?
4. *The Great Dictator* or *Black Narcissus*?
5. *Ghandi* or *Beetlejuice*?
6. *Kes* or *The Odd Couple*?
7. *The Conjuring* or *Spotlight*?
8. *North By Northwest* or *Guys and Dolls*?
9. *Awakenings* or *The Firm*?
10. *The Exorcist* or *The Wicker Man*?
11. *Girl with a Pearl Earring* or *The Village*?
12. *Pretty Woman* or *My Left Foot*?
13. *Children of the Damned* or *Patton*?
14. *Arrival* or *Fantastic Beasts: Crimes of Grindelwald*?
15. *Fame* or *Time Bandits*?

Answers – Chicken or Egg

1. *Dune* in 1984, *Roger Rabbit* was 1988
2. *The King's Speech* in 2010, *The Book Thief* was 2013
3. *The Zodiac Killer* was 1971, *The Towering Inferno* was 1974
4. *The Great Dictator* in 1940, *Black Narcissus* was 1947
5. *Ghandi* in 1982, *Beetlejuice* was 1988
6. *The Odd Couple* in 1968, *Kes* was 1969
7. *The Conjuring* in 2013, *Spotlight* was 2015
8. *Guys and Dolls* in 1955, *North By Northwest* was 1959
9. *Awakenings* in 1990, *The Firm* was 1993
10. They were both released in 1973
11. *Girl With a Pearl Earring* was 2003, *The Village* was 2004
12. *My Left Foot* in 1989, *Pretty Woman* was 1990
13. *Children of the Damned* in 1964, *Patton* was 1970
14. *Arrival* in 2016, *Fantastic Beasts: CoG* was 2018
15. *Fame* in 1980, *Time Bandits* was 1981

Famous Last Lines

These are the famous last lines of films, can you name them.

1. Now, where was I? (Guy Pearce)
2. This is Ripley, last survivor of the Nostromo, signing off (Sigourney Weaver)
3. I'm too old for this (Mel Gibson)
4. Hang on lads; I've got a great idea (Michael Caine)
5. That'll do pig. That'll do (James Cromwell)
6. You know somethin', Ultvich? I think this might just be my masterpiece (Brad Pitt)
7. Son of a b***h…stole my line (Robin Williams)
8. So long…partner (Tom Hanks, voice)
9. What about the person we show it to? What happens to them? (David Dorfman)
10. I never had any friends later on like the ones I had when I was twelve. Jesus does anyone? (Richard Dreyfuss)

Answers – Famous Last Lines

1. *Memento*
2. *Alien*
3. *Lethal Weapon*
4. *The Italian Job*
5. *Babe*
6. *Inglourious Basterds*
7. *Good Will Hunting*
8. *Toy Story 3*
9. *The Ring*
10. *Stand By Me*

Find the Links Again

1. *The War of the Roses, Junior, Twins, Matilda*
2. *Never Let Me Go, Promising Young Woman, Pride & Prejudice*
3. *Cinderella (2021), Everybody's Talking About Jamie, One Night in Miami…, Sound of Metal*
4. *Iron Man, The Da Vinci Code, Wimbledon, A Knight's Tale*
5. *Easy Rider, A Few Good Men, One Flew Over the Cuckoo's Nest, The Departed*
6. *Cujo, Children of the Corn, Firestarter, The Running Man*
7. *The Day After Tomorrow, Twister, 2012, Cloudy with a Chance of Meatballs*
8. *Boyz n the Hood, If Beale Street Could Talk, Daddy Day Care and Miss Congeniality 2: Armed and Fabulous*
9. *Rumor Has It…, Labyrinth, Just Married, Terminator*
10. *The Witches, Rio, Ocean's 8, The Devil Wears Prada*

Answers- Find the Links Again

1. Danny DeVito
2. Carey Mulligan
3. They are Amazon Prime Original Films
4. Paul Bettany
5. Jack Nicholson
6. All based on Stephen King novels
7. They are all about extreme weather events
8. Angela Bassett
9. The main female lead is called Sarah
10. Anne Hathaway

Printed in Great Britain
by Amazon